My Password Vault

Sans Sargent

ISBN:9781511885324

Glendower Media
Whitmore Lake and Toronto

DEDICATION

For all of us who gather so many programs, apps, games and products. We all have to have the password and we need to have them handy. This is for not losing or forgetting them.

Bringing security to your computer and to your programs

The reason for this book.....

Every other day, it seems, we hear of some large store or bank who has been hacked and the passwords and user names have been exposed. Now more than any other time in history, protection and remembering your passwords is vital to living in this internet driven world. Security is only one part of the puzzle. You also have to remember dozens of separate passwords to run programs, bank and financial information, apps, and website access. In addition some sites require you to change passwords and use both old and new passwords to regain access. How to you remember them all?

You put them where you can get them, where people can't easily get hold of them and where you can add and update easily. That place is NOT your computer. You need a safe and secure place in your home or office to contain your passwords and user names. Some people use this book by type of program or site. For example one page for Social Media, one for websites and other pages for programs. Be sure not to remove old passwords as they may be needed to retrieve information from old sites.

Security is easy if you plan. Make your life easier and keep passwords close to you.

My Password Vault

Program	User Name	Password

Notes:

Notes

My Password Vault

Program	User Name	Password

Notes:

My Password Vault

Program	User Name	Password

Notes:

My Password Vault

Program	User Name	Password

Notes:

My Password Vault

Program	User Name	Password

Notes:

My Password Vault

Program	User Name	Password

Notes:

My Password Vault

Program	User Name	Password

Notes:

My Password Vault

Program	User Name	Password

Notes:

My Password Vault

Program	User Name	Password

Notes:

My Password Vault

Program	User Name	Password

Notes:

My Password Vault

Program	User Name	Password

Notes:

My Password Vault

Program	User Name	Password

Notes:

My Password Vault

Program	User Name	Password

Notes:

My Password Vault

Program	User Name	Password

Notes:

My Password Vault

Program	User Name	Password

Notes:

My Password Vault

Program	User Name	Password

Notes:

My Password Vault

Program	User Name	Password

Notes:

My Password Vault

Program	User Name	Password

Notes:

My Password Vault

Program	User Name	Password

Notes:

My Password Vault

Program	User Name	Password

Notes:

My Password Vault

Program	User Name	Password

Notes:

My Password Vault

Program	User Name	Password

Notes:

My Password Vault

Program	User Name	Password

Reminders

Change passwords on an irregular basis. Not monthly or weekly but on a random but timely basis. This is to prevent hackers "Fishing" for new passwords.

Strong passwords contain numbers, letters and symbols. Some sites do not allow symbols so be sure to check the proper protocol for each website.

Security and safety of your passwords is YOUR responsibility. Do not trust your computer to remember. Hackers like to find lists of passwords on computers. It makes their lives easier.

My Password Vault

Program	User Name	Password

Notes:

My Password Vault

Program	User Name	Password

Notes:

My Password Vault

Program	User Name	Password

Notes:

My Password Vault

Program	User Name	Password

Notes:

My Password Vault

Program	User Name	Password

Notes:

My Password Vault

Program	User Name	Password

Notes:

My Password Vault

Program	User Name	Password

Notes:

My Password Vault

Program	User Name	Password

Notes:

My Password Vault

Program	User Name	Password

Notes:

My Password Vault

Program	User Name	Password

Notes:

My Password Vault

Program	User Name	Password

Notes:

My Password Vault

Program	User Name	Password

Notes:

My Password Vault

Program	User Name	Password

Notes:

My Password Vault

Program	User Name	Password

Notes:

My Password Vault

Program	User Name	Password

Notes:

My Password Vault

Program	User Name	Password

Notes:

My Password Vault

Program	User Name	Password

Notes:

My Password Vault

Program	User Name	Password

Notes:

My Password Vault

Program	User Name	Password

Notes:

My Password Vault

Program	User Name	Password

Notes:

My Password Vault

Program	User Name	Password

Notes:

My Password Vault

Program	User Name	Password

Notes:

My Password Vault

Program	User Name	Password

Notes:

My Password Vault

Program	User Name	Password

Notes:

My Password Vault

Program	User Name	Password

Notes:

www.ingramcontent.com/pod-product-compliance
Lightning Source LLC
Chambersburg PA
CBHW061037050326
40689CB00012B/2876
* 9 7 8 1 5 1 1 8 8 5 3 2 4 *